WORTHY!
THE SONG OF THE AGES
AN EASTER CELEBRATION FOR ANY CHOIR

MARTY PARKS

lillenas
PUBLISHING COMPANY

lillenas.com

Contents

~ I ~
WORTHY OF PRAISE

Holy! Worthy

with

Worthy Is the Lamb

Words and Music by
MARTY PARKS
Arr. by Marty Parks

*NARRATOR: After this I looked, and there before me was a door standing open in heaven. In the center, around the throne, were four living creatures. Day and night they never stop saying: "Holy, holy, holy is the Lord God Almighty, who was, and is, and is to come." *(Rev. 4:1a, 6b, 8b)*

*NARRATOR: Then I saw a Lamb, looking as if it had been slain, standing in the center of the throne, encircled by the four living creatures and the elders. [They] fell down before the Lamb . . . and they sang a new song, "You are worthy to take the scroll and to open its seals, because you were slain, and with your blood you purchased men for God from every tribe and language and people and nation." *(Rev. 5:6a, 8b, 9)*

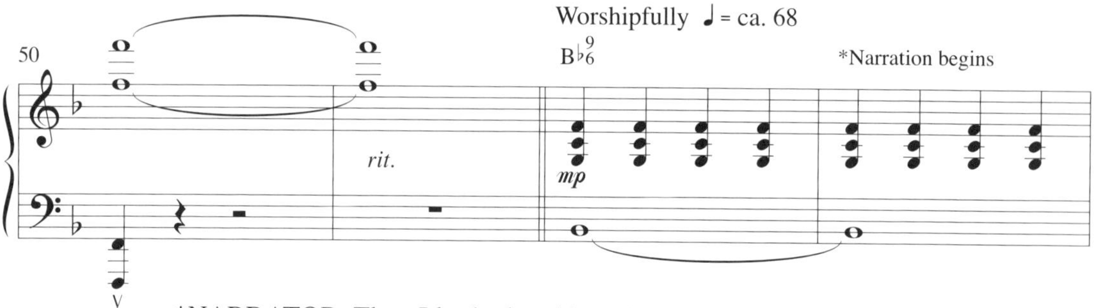

*NARRATOR: Then I looked and heard the voice of many angels, numbering thousands upon thousands, and ten thousand times ten thousand. They encircled the throne and the living creatures and the elders. In a loud voice they sang . . . *(Rev. 5:11, 12a)*

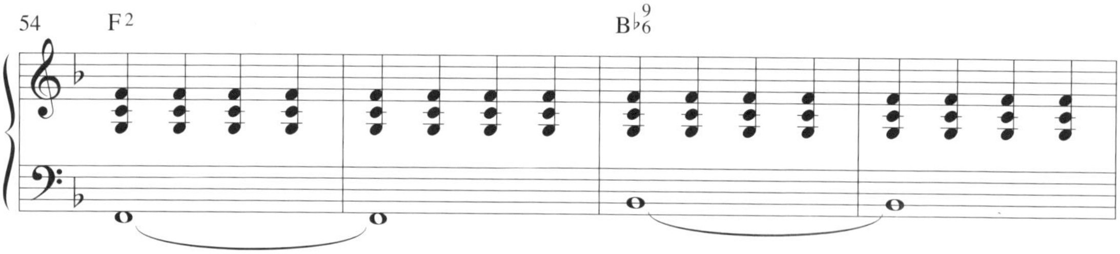

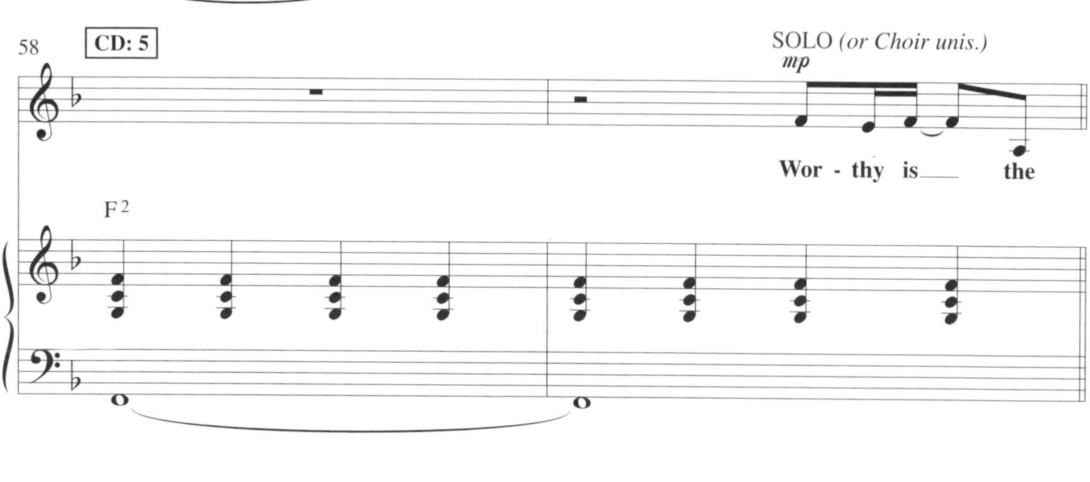

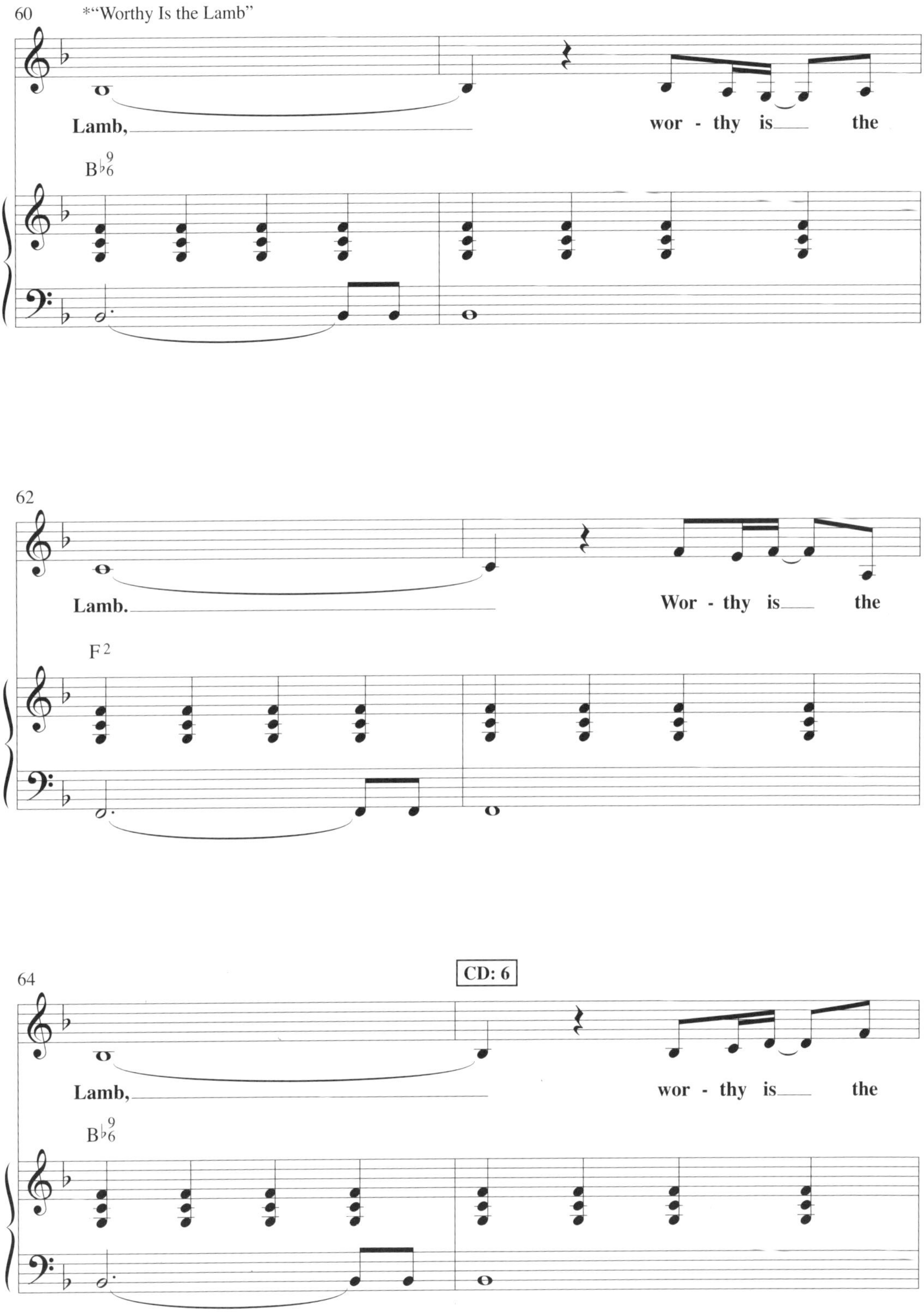
60
*"Worthy Is the Lamb"
Lamb, wor - thy is the
B♭6/9
62
Lamb. Wor - thy is the
F2
64
CD: 6
Lamb, wor - thy is the
B♭6/9

66
SOLO joins Choir
on melody, ad lib
Lamb.
CHOIR unis.
mp
Wor - thy is the
mp
C sus
F2
68
Lamb,
wor - thy is the
B♭6/9

70
Lamb.
Wor - thy is the
F2
72
Lamb,
wor - thy is the
B♭9/6
74
cresc.
mf
Lamb.
To re - ceive
Csus
A7/C♯

76
pow - er and rich - es,
D m
D m/C
78
LADIES unis.
wis - dom and strength. Wor - thy is the
B♭M7
C/B♭
F2/A
80
Lamb, Wor - thy is the
MEN unis.
Wor - thy is the Lamb,
G m7
G m7/C

*NARRATOR: Then I heard every creature in heaven and on earth and under the earth and on the sea, and all that is in them, singing: To him who sits on the throne and to the Lamb be praise and honor and glory and power for ever and ever! *(Rev. 5:13)*

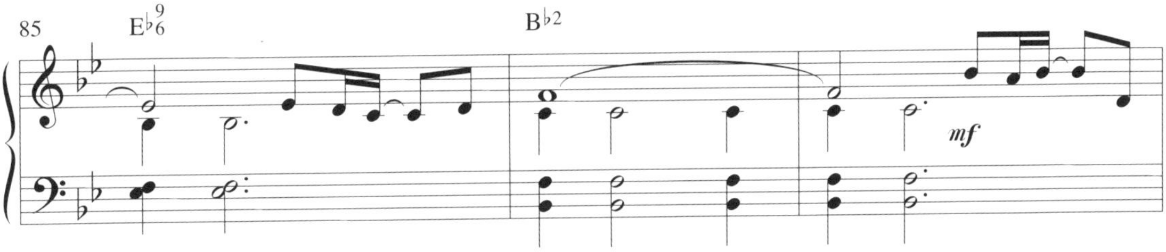

91
To re - ceive pow - er and
F sus
D 7/F♯
G m
93
rich - es, wis - dom and strength;
G m/F
E♭M7
B♭2/D
B♭/D
D 7/F♯
96
CD: 9
Hon - or and glo - ry and praise!
G m
G m/F
G m
F sus

99
rit.
a tempo
Wor - thy is the Lamb!
F sus
C/E
C
F 6 9
rit.
a tempo
8vb
101
Wor - thy is the Lamb!
F 6 9
C 2
(8vb)
8vb
103
Wor-thy is the Lamb!
Wor-thy is the
C 2
C/E
C
F 6 9
(8vb)
8vb

106
Lamb! Wor-thy is the Lamb!
G sus
C
C/B♭
109
Wor-thy is the Lamb!
ff
Wor-thy is the
Fm6/A♭
C
C/B♭
Fm6/A♭
112
Lamb!
N.C.
ff
D♭/G
C
8va
8vb

All for the Glory of His Name

Words and Music by
MELODIE TUNNEY
Arr. by Marty Parks

With dignity ♩ = ca. 78

9
Sin - less and un - blem - ished, till the work was fin - ished,
B♭ B♭/D E♭ #4 2 E♭ D D/F# G 4 2 Gm
11
CHOIR unis.
CD: 11
To re - deem His chos - en ones.
Cm7 Fsus F B♭ B♭/D E♭/B♭ #4 2 E♭/B♭
13
mp
All for the glo - ry of His name
mp
B♭ Fsus F B♭ B♭/D E♭/B♭ #4 2 E♭/B♭ B♭ Fsus F

16
To a sin - ful world He came;
MEN unis.
B♭ B♭/D E♭ B♭/E♭ F sus F
18
Per - fect love to give us mer - cy and de - liv - 'rance,
B♭ B♭/D E♭ E♭ D D/F♯ G Gm
CHOIR unis.
20
mf
For the glo - ry of His name.
C m7 F sus F B♭ B♭/D E♭ E♭

22
CD: 12
B♭ Gm7 Fsus F
C C/E F#4/2 F
Dm7 Gsus G
25
mf
All for the glo - ry of His name,
mf
C F#4/2 F
C Am Gsus G
27
May our heart and pas - sions be
C F C/F
Gsus G

29
Lived in pure de - vo - tion, as we seek to know the
C
C/E
F♯4/2
F
E
E/G♯
A4/2
Am
31
cresc.
Full - ness of a life re - deemed.
CD: 13
f
Dm7
Gsus
G
A♭
B♭
33
rit.
a tempo
All for the glo - ry
Cm
B♭/D
N.C.
E♭
E♭/G
A♭♯4/2
A♭

35
of His name, May our lives be set a - part;
E♭ Cm B♭sus B♭ E♭ E♭/G A♭ E♭/A♭ B♭sus B♭
38
All for His glo - ry! All for His hon - or!
E♭ E♭/G A♭♯4 2 A♭ G G/B C4 2 Cm
41
For the glo - ry of His name;
Cm Fm7 B♭sus B♭ Cm Cm/B♭

44
For the glo - ry of His name!
Fm7 B♭7sus E♭ E♭/G A♭#4 2 A♭ G G/B C 4 2 Cm
47
For the glo - ry of His
Fm7 Fsus Fm7 B♭7sus B♭7
50
rit.
name!
E♭ E♭/G A♭#4 2 A♭ N.C. E♭
rit.

~ II ~
WORTHY OF OUR LOVE

The Love of Christ

with

My Savior's Love

Words and Music by
MARTY PARKS
Arr. by Marty Parks

*NARRATOR: Because of his great love for us, God, who is rich in mercy, made us alive with Christ even when we were dead in transgressions– it is by grace you have been saved. This is how God showed his love among us: He sent his one and only Son into the world that we might live through him. This is love: not that we loved God, but that he loved us and sent his Son as an atoning sacrifice for our sins. And I pray that you, being rooted and established in love, may have power, together with all the saints, to grasp how wide and long and high and deep is the love of Christ. *(Eph. 2:4, 5; 1 John 4:9, 10; Eph. 3:17b-18)*

9
12
CD: 15
15
SOLO
mp
18
How long,
how wide,
how deep,
21
how high
is the love
of Christ,

24
the love of Christ. How long,
27
how wide, how deep, how high
B♭2
Dm7
Fm
30
is the love of Christ, the love of
B♭7
E♭M7
N.C.
B♭/F
F7
E♭/F
33
CD: 16
Christ.
B♭2
E♭M7
C2
mf

36
CHOIR unis.
mf
How long, how wide, how deep,
mf
FM7/G
C
C2
Em
Em7
39
how high is the love of Christ,
Gm7
C7
C9
FM9
F6
42
LADIES unis.
the love of Christ.
How long,
F6
C/G
G9
G13

*Words and Music by CHARLES H. GABRIEL. Arr.

54
presence Of Jesus, the Nazarene, And
F C7/F Gm/F F Gm7 F9/A
57
wonder how He could love me, A
B♭ B°7 F2/C F/C Dm7 D♭°7
59
CD: 18
sinner, condemned, unclean.
F/C Gm/C C7 F B♭/C C7 B♭M7/C
cresc.

61
mf
How mar - vel - ous! How won - der - ful!
mf
F Gm/F F Gm/F F
mf
63
And my song shall ev - er be: How mar-vel-ous!
Gm C7 Gm7 Dm7 C7 F Gm/F F
66
How won-der-ful Is my Sav - ior's love for
F Gm/F F Gm/B♭ Am Gm6 F/C Gm/C F/C C7

CD: 19
me! When with the ran-somed in
glo - ry His face I at last shall see, 'Twill
be my joy thro' the a - ges To sing, sing of His
mel.
cresc.
f

CD: 20
78
love, His love for me!
D7sus D7 G Am/D N.C.
8vb
81
How mar-vel-ous! How won-der-ful! And my song shall
G Am/G G Am/G G Am D7
84
ev - er be: How mar-vel-ous! How won-der-ful
Am7 Em7 D7 G Am/G G Am/G G

87
CD: 21
Is my Sav - ior's love for me!
Am/C Bm Am6 G/D Am/D G/D D7 E♭ D♭/E♭ E♭ D♭/E♭ E♭
90
How mar - vel - ous! How won - der - ful!
A♭ A♭/C
92
And my song shall ev - er be: How mar-vel-ous!
B♭m E♭7 B♭m7 Fm7 E♭7 A♭ B♭m/A♭ A♭

95
How wonder-ful Is my Sav-ior's love,
A♭ B♭m/A♭ A♭ B♭m/D♭ Cm B♭m6 A♭ B♭m/D♭ A♭/E♭
98
Is my Sav-ior's love, Is my
B♭m/D♭ Cm B♭m6 A♭ B♭m/D♭ Fm7 B♭m/D♭ Cm B♭m6
101
Sav - ior's love for
mf
A♭ B♭m/D♭ A♭/E♭ E♭7

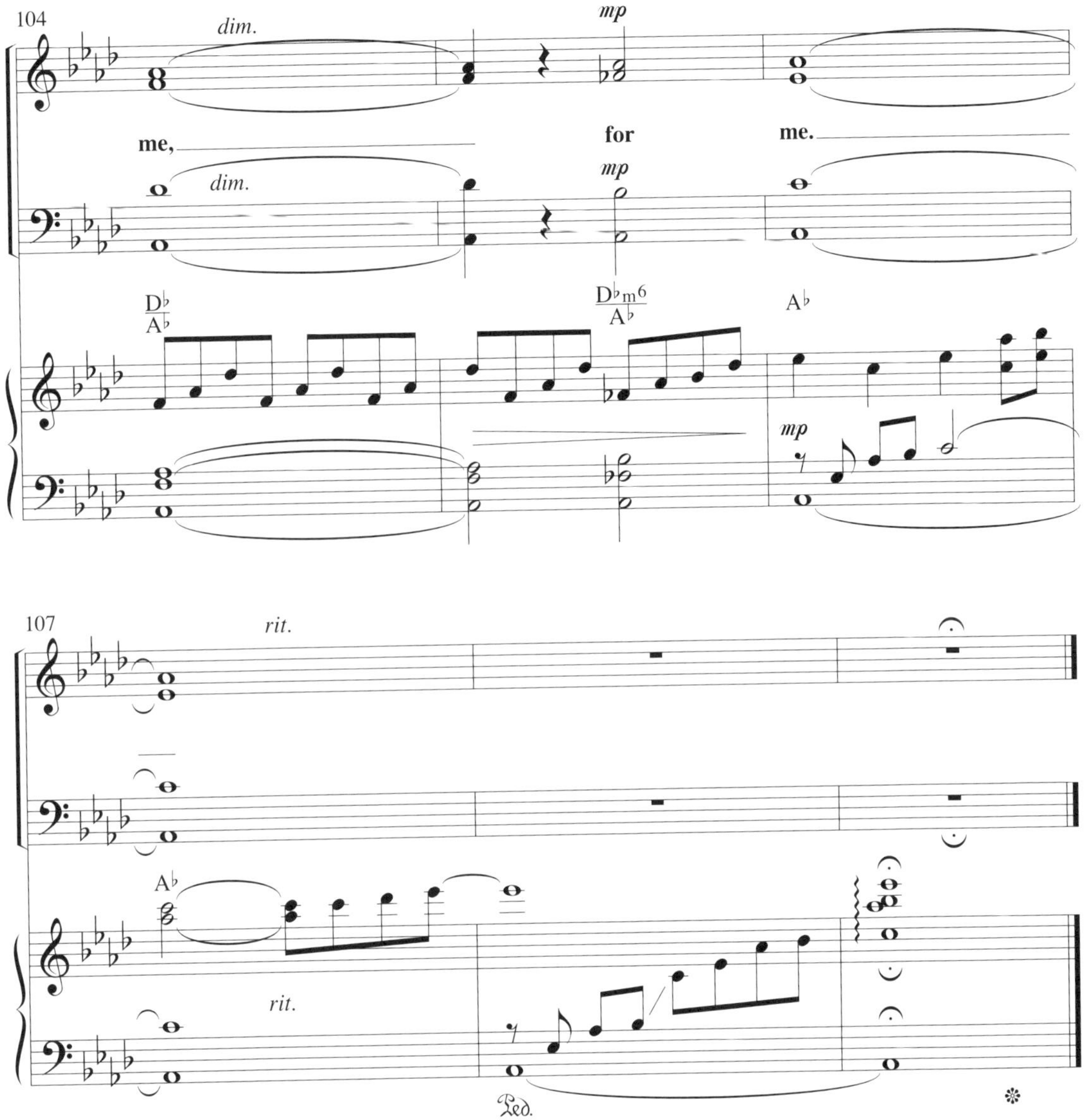

(Without music)

NARRATOR: It was just before the Passover Feast. Jesus knew that the time had come for him to leave this world and go to the Father. Having loved his own who were in the world, he now showed them the full extent of his love. When the hour came, Jesus and his apostles reclined at the table. He said to them, "I have eagerly desired to eat this Passover with you before I suffer. For I tell you, I will not eat it again until it finds fulfillment in the kingdom of God."

The Lord Jesus, on the night he was betrayed, took bread, and when he had given thanks, he broke it and said, "This is my body, which is for you; do this in remembrance of me." *(John 13:1; Luke 22:14-16; 1 Cor. 11:23b-24)*

(Music begins)

I Remember You

with

Nothing but the Blood

Words and Music by
CHRISTINE HAYS
Arr. by Marty Parks

Reflectively, in two 𝅗𝅥 = ca. 52

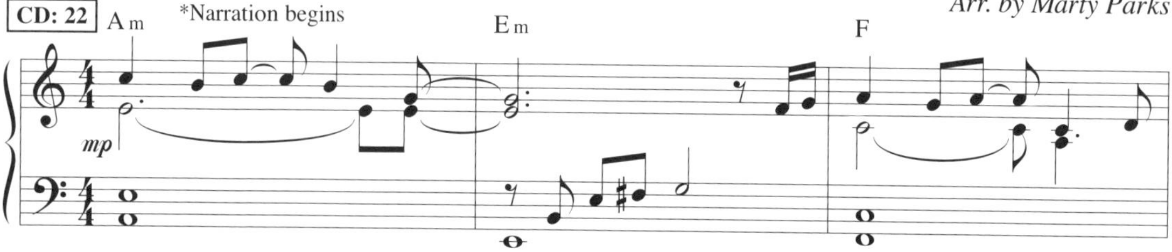

*NARRATOR: In the same way, after supper he took the cup, saying, This cup is the new covenant in my blood; do this, whenever you drink it, in remembrance of me. For whenever you eat this bread and drink this cup, you proclaim the Lord's death until he comes. *(1 Cor. 11:25-26)*

10
bread, bro - ken for me. And I
C2/E F G Am
13
thank You, Lord, for all You've done.
Dm G9/B C Am7 B♭
16
I take this cup,
F6/G C Dm7 C2/E C/E

19
spilled from Your side; You took my shame,
F Dm7 G
Am
Em
22
You called my name; So to -
Am7
Em
Am7
25
day I re - mem - ber You;
Dm
C/D Dm
F/G
G G7
Am

CD: 23
28
So to - day I re - mem - ber
Am/G Dm C/D Dm F/G G G7
31
f
You. I re - mem -
C F
34
ber Your sac - ri - fice, How You
G/F G9/F Em Am

37
paid the price that I should have paid.
Dm7
C2/E
Gsus
40
I re - mem - ber how You
G
C
C7
F
G
G/F
E7sus
E7
43
LADIES unis.
mf
gave Your life; How You died for me,
Am
CM7/G
F
C2/E
mf

*Words and Music by ROBERT LOWRY. Arr.

55
That makes me white as snow.
F
F
A
Gm N.C.
58
No oth - er fount I know–
F
F
E♭
G
D
Am9
G
B
Bm
CM7
61
CD: 25
Noth - ing but the blood,
Noth - ing but the blood,
G
D
GM7
D
Am
D
Am7
D

63
rit.
Noth-ing but the blood of Je - sus. I re -
G M7/D
C/D
D7sus
D7
C/D
rit.
66
a tempo
mem - ber Your sac - ri-fice, How You
G
A/G
A9/G
F♯m
B m
a tempo
70
paid the price that I should have paid.
E m7
D2/F♯
F♯m7
B m/F♯
A sus
3

73
I re - mem - ber how You
A
D/F♯
G
A
A/G
F♯7sus F♯7
76
gave Your life; How You died for me,
Bm
DM7/A
G
D2/F♯
79
CD: 26
There cru - ci - fied for me. That
G2
D2/F♯
G2

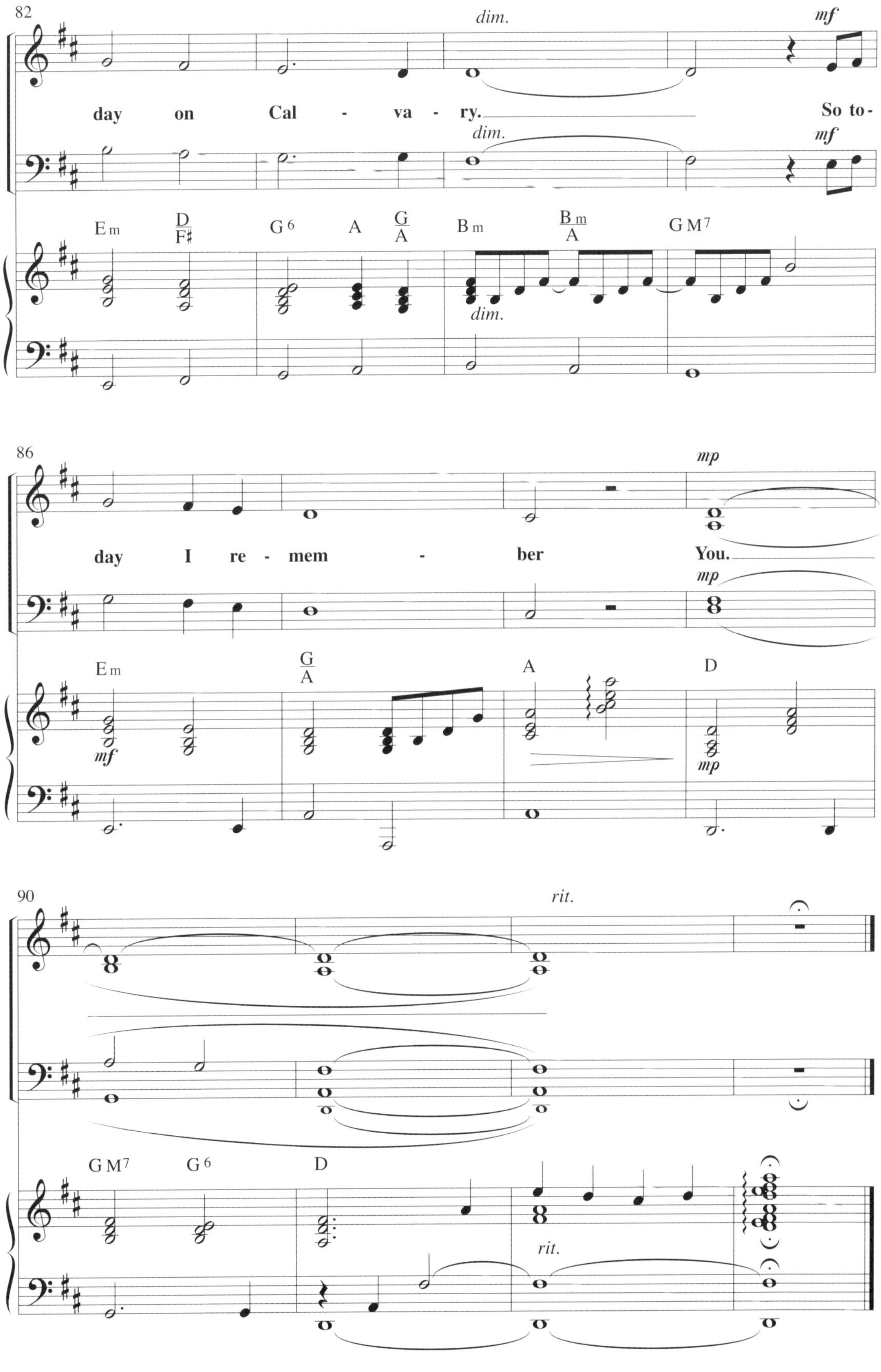
82
dim.
mf
day on Cal - va - ry.
So to -
dim.
mf
Em D/F♯ G6 A G/A Bm Bm/A GM7
dim.
86
mp
day I re - mem - ber You.
mp
Em G/A A D
mf
mp
90
rit.
GM7 G6 D
rit.

I Will Sing of My Redeemer

PHILIP P. BLISS

THOMAS J. WILLIAMS
Arr. by Marty Parks

Energetically ♩. = ca. 64

Music used by permission of Eluned Crump and Dilys Evans

16
deem - er And His won - drous
Em D/E Em G D/F♯ B+/D♯ B7/D♯ Em
19
love for me; On the
Am B7 Em Bm7 Em
22
cru - el cross He suf - fered,
B7 CM7 Am6 B7 Em D/E Em

25
CD: 28
From the curse to set me
G D/F♯ B+/D♯ B7/D♯ Em Am B7
28
free.
mel.
Sing, O sing of
f
mel.
Em D/F♯ G Dsus D
31
my Re - deem - er. With His
Em Bsus B Em Em/D

34
blood He pur - chased me.
C6 D Em Am7 B Bm7
37
On the cross He sealed my
Em B7 CM7 Am6 B7
40
par - don, Paid the debt and
Em D/E Em G D/F♯ B+/D♯ B7/D♯ Em

CD: 31
2nd time
2nd time to Coda
(to pg. 50, meas. 64)
CD: 29
made me free.
2nd time to Coda
(to pg. 50, meas. 64)
Am B7 Em D/E Em B7sus
LADIES unis.
mf
I will tell the
Bm7 Em/B Bm7 Em/B Bm7 Em B7 CM7
mf
won - drous sto - ry, How, my
Am6 B7 Em D/E Em G D/F♯

53
lost es - tate to save,
B+/D♯ B7/D♯ Em Am B7 Em
56
MEN unis.
In His bound - less love and
mf
Em B7 CM7 Am6 B7
59
mer - cy He the rans - om
Em D/E Em G D/F♯ B+/D♯ B7/D♯ Em

62
CD: 30
D.S. al Coda
(to pg. 46, meas. 29)
CODA
free - ly gave. free.
A m
B 7
E m
D/F♯
C
65
mel.
Sing, O sing of my Re -
G
D
D 7/F♯
68
deem - er. With His blood He
B sus
B/D♯
E m/D
C 6

71
CD: 32
pur - chased me.
Em Am7 Bsus B/F♯ B Csus C
74
On the cross He sealed my par - don,
Fm Fm/A♭ C7 D♭M7 B♭m6 C7 Fm E♭/F Fm
78
Paid the debt and made me
A♭ E♭/G C+/E C7/E Fm B♭m Csus C7
8vb
8vb

(Without music)

NARRATOR: Your attitude should be the same as that of Christ Jesus: Who, being in very nature God, did not consider equality with God something to be grasped, but made himself nothing, taking the very nature of a servant, being made in human likeness. And being found in appearance as a man, he humbled himself and became obedient to death–even death on a cross! *(Phil. 2:5-8)*

(Music begins)

~ III ~
A WORTHY SACRIFICE
Those Radiant Scars

Words and Music by
MARTY PARKS
Arr. by Marty Parks

*NARRATOR: He is the atoning sacrifice for our sins, and not only for ours but also for the sins of the whole world. *(1 John 2:2)*

11
deem - ing sac - ri - fice, I'm cov - ered by the blood of
A♭ B♭ G/B C m C m/B♭ C m/A E♭/A♭ E♭/B♭ B♭7
14
CD: 34
Christ.
C m A♭M7 G m7 A♭ F m7 E♭ D♭
18
mf
He had no beau - ty we could
B♭sus B♭ A♭/B♭ E♭ A♭/B♭

21
name, He had no maj - es - ty to claim; For me He
E♭ E♭2 Gm A♭2 B♭sus B♭ E♭ E♭/G
24
CD: 35
paid sin's dread - ful price, I'm cov - ered by the blood of
A♭ B♭ G/B Cm Cm/B♭ Cm/A E♭/A♭ A♭/B♭ B♭7
27
cresc.
f
Christ. I'm cov - ered by His blood, sur -
E♭sus E♭ E♭sus E♭ E♭/G Cm B♭ A♭ E♭ A♭

31
round - ed by His love; My guil - ty debt is
E♭ C m7 B♭sus B♭ C m B♭ A♭ B♭
34
paid, My sin on Him is laid. O I'm
C m F m7 E♭ B♭sus B♭ A♭/B♭ B♭
37
cov - ered by His blood, sur - round - ed by His
C m B♭ A♭ E♭ A♭ E♭ C m7

40
love.; My guil - ty debt is paid, My
B♭sus B♭ Cm B♭ A♭ B♭ Cm Fm7
43
dim.
mf
sin on Him is laid. O hal - le -
E♭ B♭sus B♭
46
CD: 36
lu - jah, O hal - le - lu - jah.
A♭6 A♭ E♭/G A♭6 A♭ A♭/B♭

50
rit.
mp
a tempo
Then how can I, in His em - brace, Re - ceive His
A♭/B♭
N.C.
mp a tempo
53
cresc.
mf
mer - cy, own His grace? No oth - er plead - ing will suf -
E♭ E♭/G A♭ B♭ G/B
56
dim.
fice I'm cov - ered by the blood of Christ.
Cm Cm/B♭ Cm/A E♭/B♭ E♭/B♭ B♭7 Cm Cm/B♭

(Without music)

NARRATOR: God made him who had no sin to be sin for us, so that in him we might become the righteousness of God. You see, just at the right time, when we were still powerless, Christ died for the ungodly. But God demonstrates his own love for us in this: While we were still sinners, Christ died for us. *(2 Cor. 5:21; Rom. 5:6, 8)*

(Music begins)

Lord, Have Mercy

Words and Music by
NATHAN DIGESARE
and DAN SCOTT
Arr. by Marty Parks

Reverently ♩= ca. 72

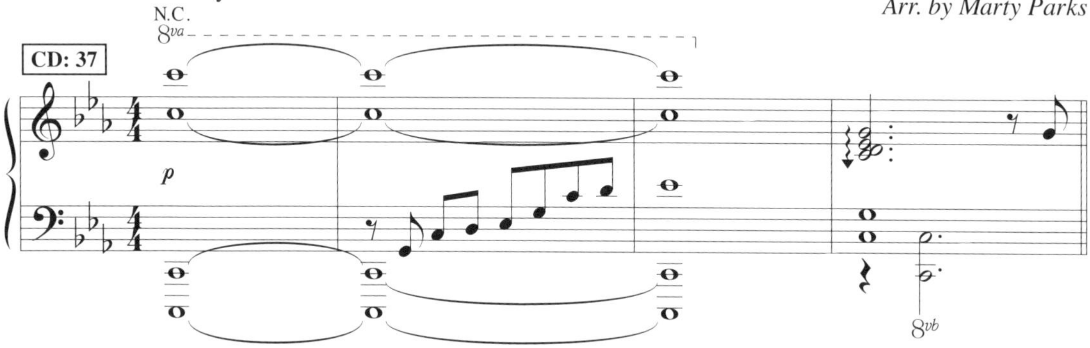

*NARRATOR: He was despised and rejected by men, a man of sorrows, and familiar with suffering. Like one from whom men hide their faces he was despised, and we esteemed him not. Surely he took up our infirmities and carried our sorrows, yet we considered him stricken by God, smitten by him, and afflicted. But he was pierced for our transgressions, he was crushed for our iniquities; the punishment that brought us peace was upon him, and by his wounds we are healed. *(Isa. 53:3-5)*

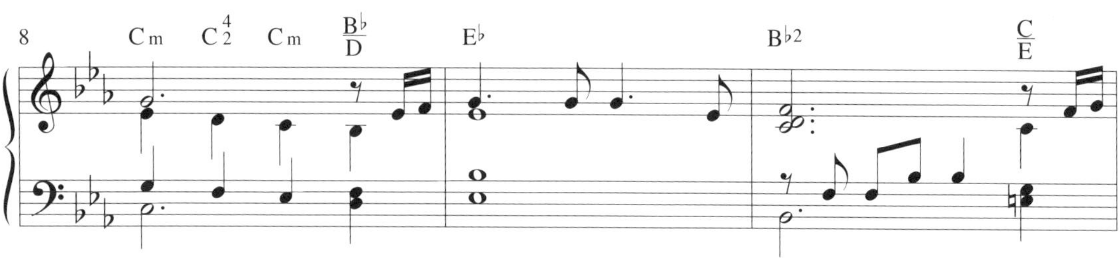

11
Fm2 Fm Cm2 Cm B♭/D E♭2
14
E♭2
cresc.
CD: 38
G/D G G7
mp
dim.
17
CHOIR unis.
p
Lord, have mer - cy, Lord, have
Cm B♭4/2 B♭ Fm F4/2/G Fm/A♭
20
mer - cy; For we have placed all our
C4/2 Cm B♭/D E♭2 E♭ B♭2 B♭/D C/E

23
hopes in Thee. Lord, have
Fm2 B♭7/D E♭2 Cm
26
mer - cy, Lord, have mer - cy;
B♭4/2 B♭ Fm F4/2/G Fm/A♭ C4/2 Cm B♭/D
29
(,)
CD: 39
For we have placed all our hopes in
E♭2 E♭ B♭2 B♭/D C/E Fm2 B♭7/D

32
mp
Thee. For our sin we re-pent, O
mp
E♭2 E♭ C m
mp
34
Lord; We be - lieve Your ho - ly Word. Have
B♭ F m C m B♭/D
37
mer - cy, Lord, we pray, And take all our sins a -
E♭ E♭sus B♭ B♭/D C/E F m

*An ancient prayer from church liturgy. Kyrie - Lord; Christe - Christ.

49
For we have placed all our hopes in
(,)
E♭ B♭ B♭/D C/E Fm2 Fm B♭7/D
52
Lord, have mer - cy,
Thee. O Lord, have mer - cy,
E♭2 E♭ Cm B♭4 2 B♭
55
Lord, have mer - cy;
O Lord, have mer - cy; For we have
Fm F4 2/G Fm/A♭ C4 2 Cm B♭/D E♭

58
CD: 41
placed all our hopes in Thee.
B♭
B♭/D
C/E
Fm2
Fm
B♭7/D
E♭
61
f
If You would mark in - iq - ui - ty, O
Cm
B♭/C
Cm
Cm/B♭
63
CD: 42
Lord, who could stand?
Mer - cy, like a
A♭
D♭

66
foun - tain, flows from Your hand!
D♭/F D♭2/F D♭/F G sus G
8vb
69
Lord, have mer - cy, Lord, have
Cm B♭4/2 B♭ Fm F4/2/G Fm/A♭
(8vb)
72
mer - cy; For we have placed all our
C4/2 Cm B♭/D E♭ B♭ B♭/D C/E
8vb

75
hopes in Thee. Lord, have
Fm F4/2 Fm/D Cm
(8vb)
78
mer - cy, Lord, have mer - cy;
Bb4/2 Bb Fm F4/2/G Fm/Ab C4/2 Cm Bb/D
8vb
81
CD: 43
(,)
For we have placed all our hopes in
Eb Bb Bb/D C/E Fm F4/2 Fm/D
(8vb)
8vb

Opt. SOLO voice
84
mp
O Lord, have mer - cy,
Thee.
Lord, have mer - cy,
mp
mp
Cm
B♭ 4 2
B♭
mp
(8vb)
87
O Lord, have mer - cy;
For we have
Lord, have mer - cy;
For we have
Fm
F 4 2 / G
Fm / A♭
C 4 2
Cm
B♭ / D
E♭

90
CD: 44
placed all our hopes in Thee.
placed all our hopes in Thee.
B♭ B♭/D C/E Fm2 Fm B♭7/D E♭2 E♭

93
Softly, almost a whisper
p
Lord, have mer - cy, Lord, have
Cm B♭4/2 B♭ Fm F4/2/G Fm/A♭

96
mer - cy; For we have
C 4 2
C m
B♭ D
E♭2
E♭
98
(,)
placed all our hopes in
B♭2
B♭ D
C E
F m2
B♭7 D
100
rit.
Thee.
E♭2
E♭
rit.

Worship at the Foot of the Cross

includes

There Is a Fountain

Who Can Satisfy My Soul

Mighty to Save

Arr. by Marty Parks

*NARRATOR: He does not treat us as our sins deserve or repay us according to our iniquities. As far as the east is from the west, so far has he removed our transgressions from us. On that day a fountain will be opened to the house of David and the inhabitants of Jerusalem, to cleanse them from sin and impurity.
(Psalm 103:10, 12; Zech. 13:1)

PLEASE NOTE: Copying of this product is NOT covered by CCLI licenses. For CCLI information call 1-800-234-2446.

*Words by WILLIAM COWPER; Music Traditional American Melody. Arr.

16
CD: 46
mf
all their guilt - y stains,
Lose
mf
B♭2
Cm/F
Dm/F
B♭2
E♭2/B♭
Gm/F
Cm/F
19
mel.
all their guilt - y stains,
Lose
B♭2
A♭/B♭
B♭
E♭2
E♭M7
mf
21
all their guilt - y stains.
And
B♭2
F
B♭/E♭

23
sin - ners, plunged be - neath that flood, Lose
mel.
B♭2
E♭2/B♭
B♭2
25
CD: 47
all their guilt - y stains.
There's a
B♭2
Cm/F
Dm/F
B♭2
E♭2/B♭
28
CHOIR unis.
mf
foun - tain!
The dy - ing thief re -
mf
B♭2
E♭2/B♭
B♭

31
joiced to see That fountain in his day; And
E♭/B♭ B♭ F/B♭ B♭/E♭
34
CD: 48
there may I, tho' vile as he, Wash all my sins a -
B♭ E♭/B♭ B♭ B♭2 B♭/F F F6
37
way, Wash all my sins a - way, Wash
B♭ E♭ B♭ A♭/B♭ B♭ E♭

40
all my sins a - way. And there may I, tho'
B♭ B♭2 F E♭/F E♭M7 B♭
43
CD: 49
vile as he, Wash all my sins a - way,
E♭/B♭ B♭ B♭2 B♭/F F F6 B♭
46
♩ = 𝅗𝅥 *"Who Can Satisfy My Soul"
There is a foun - tain
E♭/B♭ E♭ F ♩ = 𝅗𝅥 B♭

49
who is the King, Vic - to - r'ous War -
G m
E♭
52
- rior, and Lord of ev - 'ry - thing. My Rock, my Shel-
B♭
C m7 D m7 E♭ D m7
G m
C
F
B♭
56
- ter, my ver - y own;
B♭
G m

59
CD: 50
Bless - ed Re - deem - er who reigns up -
E♭ B♭ Cm7 Dm7
8vb
62
on the throne!
There is a foun -
E♭ F B♭sus B♭ F/G C
(8vb)
(Optional cued notes)
66
- tain who is the King,
G/B Am G

69
Vic - to - r'ous War - rior, and Lord of ev - 'ry -
F C C/E Dm7 Em F Em
8vb
72
thing. My Rock, my Shel - ter,
Dm7 G C
(8vb)
75
my ver - y own; Bless - ed Re - deem -
Am Am/G F

78
- er who reigns up - on the
C
C/E
Dm7
Em
F
F/G
G
8vb
81
CD: 51
accel.
throne!
Csus
C
Dsus
D
accel.
8vb
85
With joy! ♩ = ca. 70
𝅗𝅥 = ♩
f
*"Mighty to Save"
Sav - ior, He can move the moun - tains; My God is
f
G
D

87
might - y to save. He is might - y to save! For -
mel.
C G Em D
89
ev - er, Au - thor of sal - va - tion; He rose and
G D
91
CD: 52
con - quered the grave! Je - sus con - quered the grave!
mel.
C G Em D

93
mel.
Sav - ior, He can move the moun - tains; My God is
G
D
95
might - y to save. He is might - y to save! For -
C
G
Em
D
97
ev - er, Au - thor of sal - va - tion; He rose and
G
D

CD: 53
99
con-quered the grave! Je - sus con-quered the grave!
C G Em D Em
101
Shine Your light and let the whole world see; We're sing-ing
C G D Em
103
for the glo - ry of the ris - en King! Je - sus,
C G D D/E Em7

105
shine Your light and let the whole world see; We're sing-ing
C G D Em
107
for the glo - ry of the ris - en King!
C G D
109
For the glo - ry of the ris - en King! Sing - ing
C G D D/E Em7

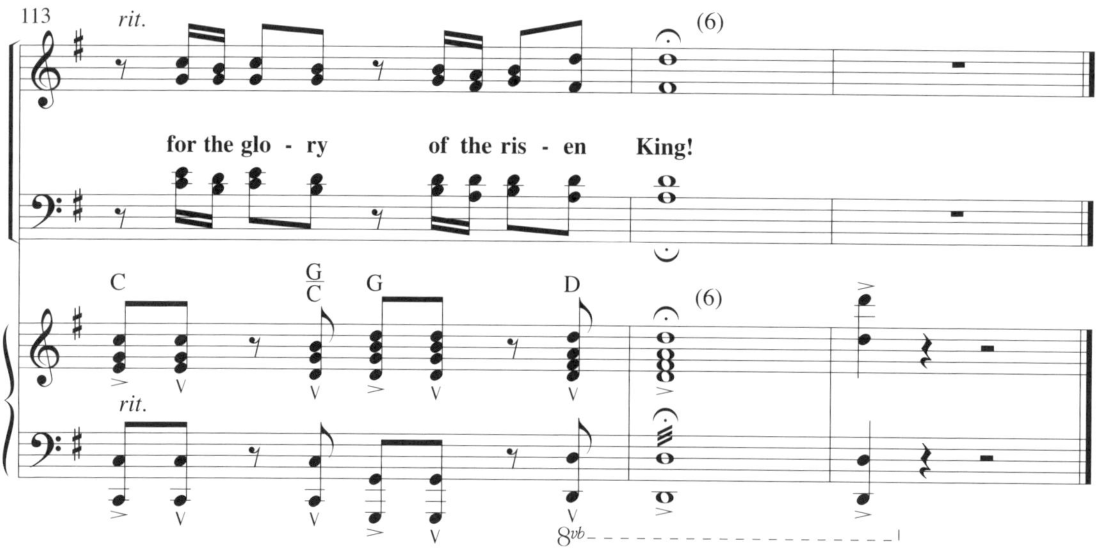

(Without music)

NARRATOR: After the Sabbath, at dawn on the first day of the week, Mary Magdelene and the other Mary went to look at the tomb. *(Matt. 28:1)*

(Music begins)

~ IV ~
WORTHY OF EXALTATION

Worthy Is the Risen King

Words and Music by
REBECCA J. PECK
Arr. by Marty Parks

Softly intense ♩ = ca. 132

*NARRATOR: There was a violent earthquake, for an angel of the Lord came down from heaven and, going to the tomb, rolled back the stone and sat on it. His appearance was like lightning, and his clothes were white as snow. The guards were so afraid of him that they shook and became like dead men. The angel said to the women, Do not be afraid, for I know that you are looking for Jesus, who was crucified. He is not here; he has risen, just as he said. Come and see the place where he lay. *(Matt. 28:2-6)*

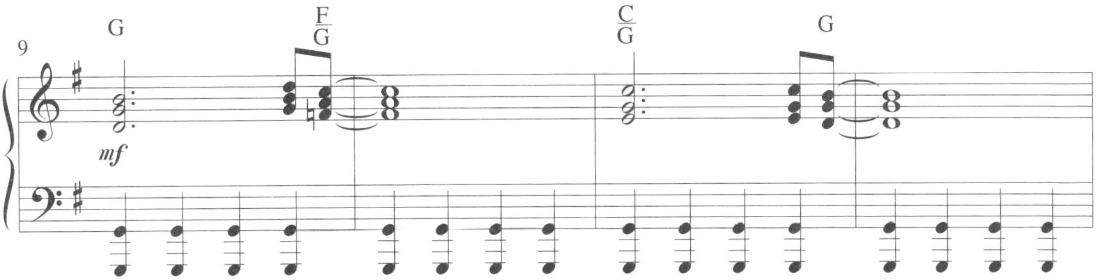

CD: 55
LADIES unis.
Lift up a joy - ous shout! The
tomb could nev - er hold Him down; The Sav - ior has
G
F/G
C
D7sus
G2
F6
F

26
ris - en as He said.
C
G2
F C
29
MEN unis. mf
Look and see His emp - ty grave, the stone has now been rolled
G2
F6
C
32
CD: 56
a - way. Je - sus has tri - umphed o - ver death!
G2
F F♯4
C C/E Dsus

35
cresc.
f
Wor - thy is the Ris -
D sus
D
D/C
B♭
38
- en King!
Sing the glo - rious vic - to - ry:
F/A
A♭
E♭/G
41
Sin has been de - feat - ed by our liv - ing Lord!
C m7
B♭2
B♭
A♭
C m/G

44
Hal - le - lu - jah! Praise His name!
F sus
F
B♭
F/A
47
Join your voic - es to pro - claim: "Wor - thy is the
A♭
E♭/G
C m7
CD: 59 2nd time
2nd time to Coda
(to pg. 94, meas. 71)
CD: 57
50
King for - ev - er - more!"
2nd time to Coda
(to pg. 94, meas. 71)
B♭/D
F
E♭/F
B♭
A♭

53
LADIES unis.
mf
Come wor - ship and
C/G
C/D
D
G2
mf
56
re-joice! The pow'rs of hell have been de-stroyed. For
All the pow'rs have been de-stroyed.
MEN unis. mf
F6
C2
C/G
G
59
there in His hand He holds the keys.
He holds the
F
C2
G2

62
keys.
Sov - 'reign o - ver all that is; Au -
G2 F C G2 F6
65
thor - i - ty and strength are His.
Je - sus shall
C2 C/G G F F♯4
68
CD: 58
D.S. al Coda
(to pg. 90, meas. 37)
reign in maj - es - ty!
C C/E Dsus D D/C
D.S. al Coda
(to pg. 90, meas. 37)

71
CODA
Still with intensity!
mp
more!"
One day the grave could con -
ceal Him no long - er;
One day the stone rolled a -
way from the door.
Then He a - rose– o - ver
mf
B♭
B♭2
B♭2/A
Gm7
B♭/F
74
E♭
B♭/D
Cm7
E♭/B♭
F/A
E♭/G
76
F
Fsus/G
F/A
B♭
B♭/A
Gm7
B♭/F

CD: 60
death He had con-quered; Wor - thy is the King for-ev - er-more!
E♭ B♭/D A♭ E♭/G
F sus F F/G Dm/G C
Wor - thy is the Ris - en King!
G/C B♭/C F/C
Sing the glo - rious vic - to - ry:
8vb

87
Sin has been de - feat - ed by our liv - ing Lord!
Dm7 C2 C B♭ Dm/A
90
Hal - le - lu - jah! Praise His name!
Gsus G C G/B
93
Join your voic - es to pro - claim: "Wor - thy is the
B♭ F/A Dm7

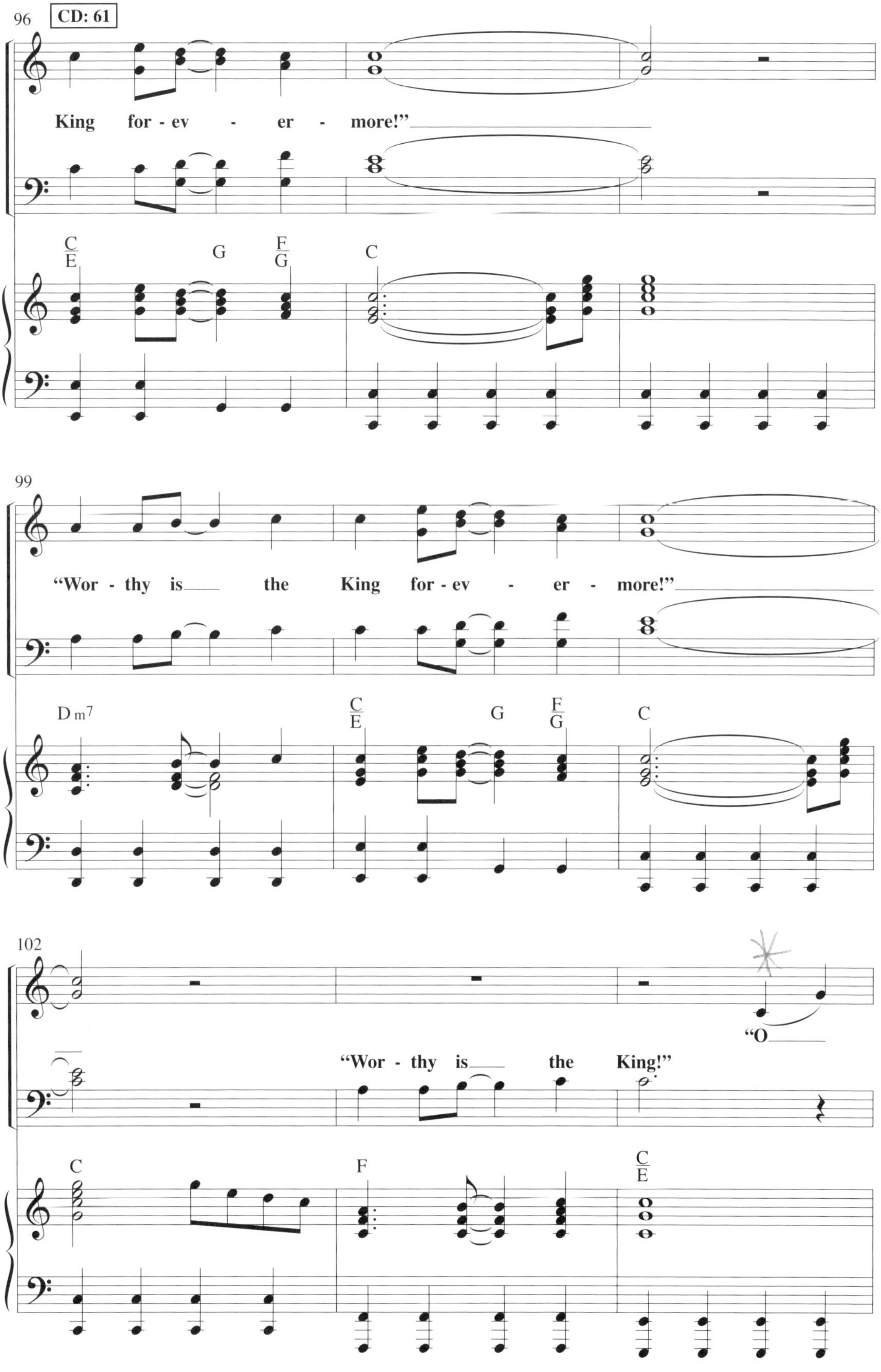
96
CD: 61
King for - ev - er - more!"
C/E G F/G C
99
"Wor - thy is the King for - ev - er - more!"
Dm7 C/E G F/G C
102
"O
"Wor - thy is the King!"
C F C/E

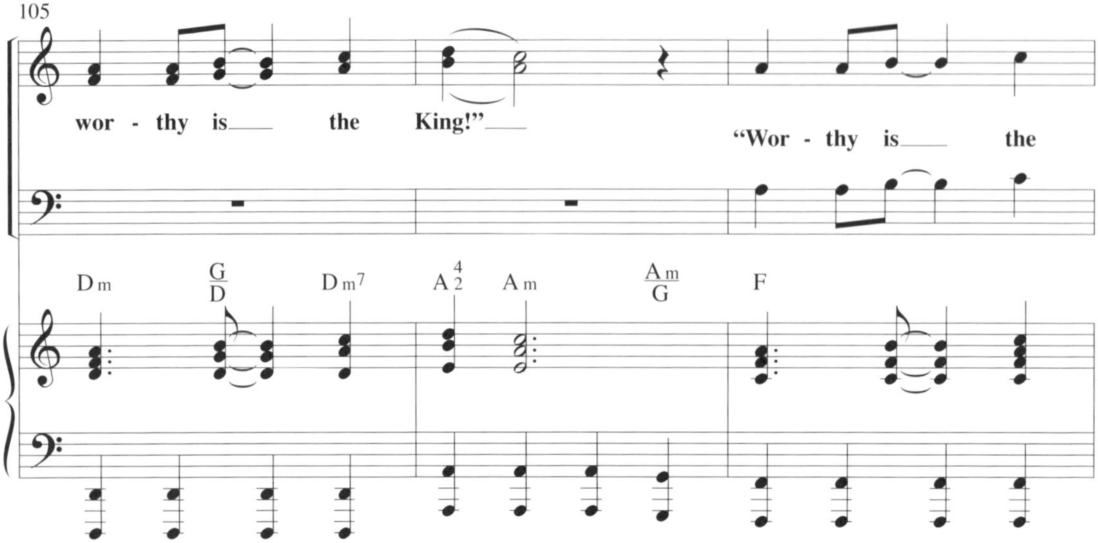

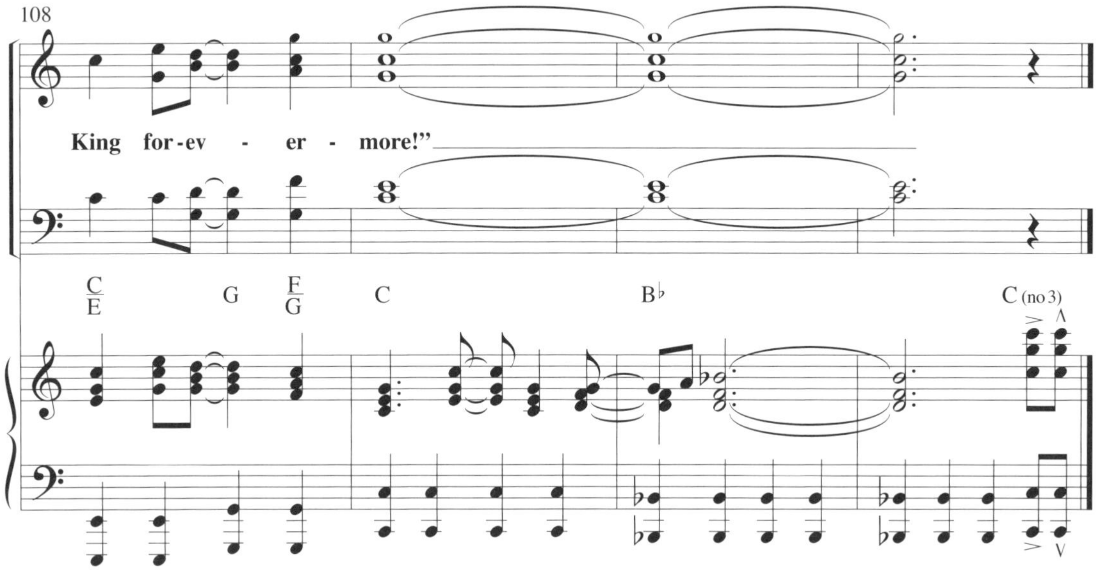

(Without music)

NARRATOR: Worthy is the Lamb, who was slain, to receive power and wealth and wisdom and strength and honor and glory and praise. *(Rev. 5:12b)*

(Music begins)

Worthy! The Song of the Ages Finale

includes

At the Name of Jesus
Crown Him with Many Crowns
Worthy Is the Lamb

Arr. by Marty Parks

*NARRATOR: But we see Jesus, who was made a little lower than the angels, now crowned with glory and honor. Let us fix our eyes on Jesus, the author and perfecter of our faith, who for the joy set before him endured the cross, scorning its shame, and sat down at the right hand of the throne of God. Therefore, God exalted him to the highest place and gave him a name that is above every name, that at the name of Jesus every knee should bow . . . and every tongue confess that Jesus Christ is Lord. *(Heb. 2:9a; 12:2; Phil. 2:9-11a)*

*Words by CAROLINE M. NOEL; Music by JAMES MOUNTAIN.

25
King of Glo - ry now.
28
CHOIR
'Tis the Fa - ther's plea - sure
31
we should call Him Lord,

34
Who from the be - gin - ning
37
CD: 64
was the might - y Word.
40
mf
Hum - bled for a sea - son
F
C
F
F
mf

43
to re-ceive a name
From the lips of
mf
B♭/F C/F F C/F
46
sin - ners un - to whom He came;
F C G/C C
49
Faith - ful - ly He bore it, spot - less to the
F B♭/F F Gm F/A Dm

52
last, Brought it back vic - tor - ious
C F A7/E Dm7 G
55
CD: 65
when from death He passed!
N.C. F/C Csus C Dsus D
57
*"Crown Him with Many Crowns"
Opt. CONGREGATION may join
Crown Him the Lord of
G/A A G/A A G/A D Bm7

59
Life! Who tri-umphed o'er the grave; Who
G D G D G D Em Bm7 A Em7 A
62
rose vic-to-rious in the strife for those He came to
(,)
D G/D D E E/G♯ A Bm A/E D/E Esus E
65
save. His glo-ries now we
A A/G D/F♯ D Em7 D/F♯

68
sing Who died and rose on high, Who
G D G G/F E Bm7 E A E A A/G
71
died e - ter - nal life to bring, And lives that
D/F♯ G D Em A D D/F♯ G Bm7
74
death may die. He died e - ter - nal
G/A A D A/G D/F♯ G D

77
life to bring and lives, He lives that death may
Em A D D/F♯ G Bm7 G/A A
80
CD: 66
rit.
die.
D D/C B♭
rit.
83
CONG. may continue
Slower ♩ = ca. 68
*"Worthy Is the Lamb"
Wor - thy is the Lamb,
E♭/F F E♭/F F B♭/D B♭ E♭6 9
Slower

85
wor - thy is the Lamb!
E♭6/9
B♭2
8vb
8vb
87
Wor - thy is the Lamb,
B♭2
E♭6/9
(8vb)
8vb
89
wor - thy is the Lamb!
E♭6/9
F sus

91
To re - ceive pow - er and
F sus
D 7/F♯
G m
93
rich - es, wis - dom and
G m/F
E♭M7
95
strength; Hon - or and
B♭2/D
B♭/D
D 7/F♯
G m

CD: 67
97
glo - ry and praise!
Gm/F
Gm
Fsus
99
rit.
Wor - thy is the Lamb!
a tempo
Fsus
C/E
F 6/9
rit.
a tempo
8vb
101
Wor - thy is the Lamb!
F 6/9
C 2
(8vb)
8vb

103
Wor - thy is the Lamb!
C2
C/E
F 6/9
(8vb)
8vb
105
Wor - thy is the Lamb!
F 6/9
G sus
107
Wor - thy is the Lamb!
G sus
C
C/B♭

109
ff
Wor-thy is the Lamb!
Wor-thy is the
Fm6/A♭
C
C/B♭
112
Lamb!
N.C.
D♭/G
8va
8vb